Bonza the Monster
and
Joan's Backyard

Level 3 – Yellow

Helpful Hints for Reading at Home

The graphemes (written letters) and phonemes (units of sound) used throughout this series are aligned with Letters and Sounds. This offers a consistent approach to learning whether reading at home or in the classroom. Books levelled as 'a' are an introduction to this band. Readers can advance to 'b' where graphemes are consolidated and further graphemes are introduced.

HERE IS A LIST OF ALTERNATIVE GRAPHEMES FOR THIS PHASE OF LEARNING. AN EXAMPLE OF THE PRONUNCIATION CAN BE FOUND IN BRACKETS.

Phase 3			
j (jug)	v (van)	w (wet)	x (fox)
y (yellow)	z (zoo)	zz (buzz)	qu (quick)
ch (chip)	sh (shop)	th (thin/then)	ng (ring)
ai (rain)	ee (feet)	igh (night)	oa (boat)
oo (boot/look)	ar (farm)	or (for)	ur (hurt)
ow (cow)	oi (coin)	ear (dear)	air (fair)
ure (sure)	er (corner)		

TOP TIPS FOR HELPING YOUR CHILD TO READ:

- Allow children time to break down unfamiliar words into units of sound and then encourage children to string these sounds together to create the word.
- Encourage your child to point out any focus phonics when they are used.
- Read through the book more than once to grow confidence.
- Ask simple questions about the text to assess understanding.
- Encourage children to use illustrations as prompts.

HERE ARE SOME WORDS WHICH YOUR CHILD MAY FIND TRICKY.

Phase 3 Tricky Words			
he	you	she	they
we	all	me	are
be	my	was	her

HERE ARE SOME WORDS THAT MIGHT NOT YET BE FULLY DECODABLE.

Challenge Words		
hear	yard	mermaid

This book is a 'b' level and is a yellow level 3 book band.

Bonza the Monster and Joan's Backyard

Written by
Kirsty Holmes

Illustrated by
Drue Rintoul

Can you say this sound and draw it with your finger?

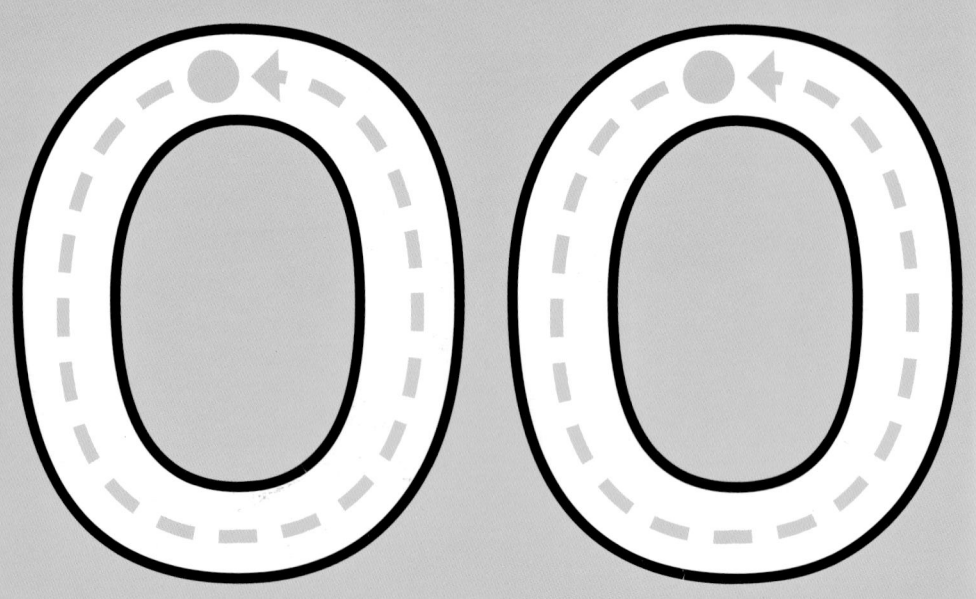

Bonza the Monster

Written by
Kirsty Holmes

Illustrated by
Drue Rintoul

I am Bonza and I am good.

This is my hut at the top of the hill.

It is good at the top, but I need a coat.

I sit on my pink mat. I am in a good mood.

This is the wool of a yak.

A hat! It will look good with my coat!

I got a medal for being good. Look!

Look at this! Is it good?

I can yell. I am good at yelling.

Did they hear me? Yes!

This is my hut. It is big and red.

Can I get you food? Can I get you a cup of tea?

Can you say this sound and draw it with your finger?

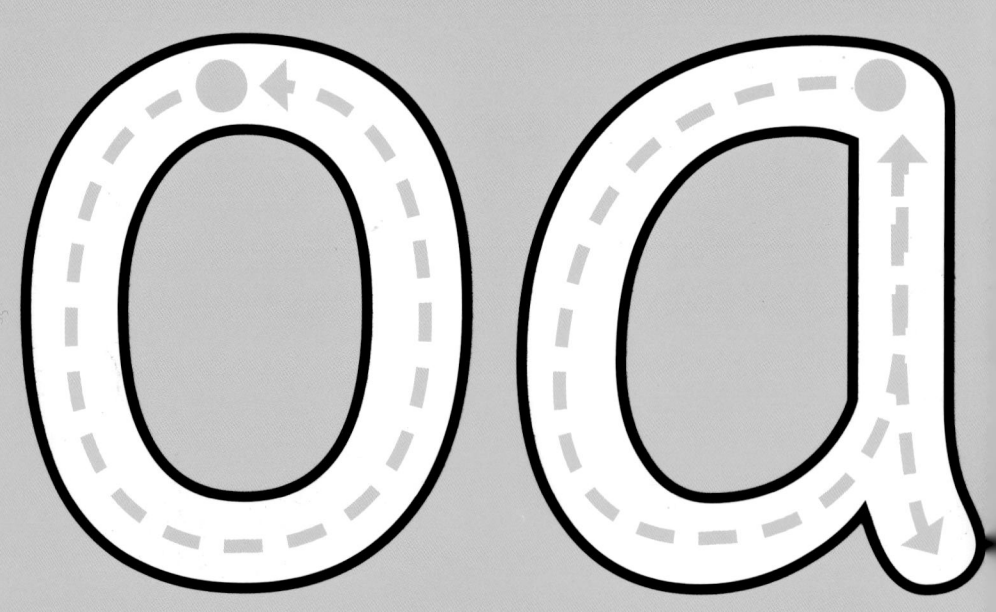

Joan's Backyard

Written by
Kirsty Holmes

Illustrated by
Drue Rintoul

Joan is set. Joan cannot wait to go.

"Not yet, Joan," yells Mum. "It is raining."

Joan will go in the backyard.

"Joan! Get a coat!" yells Mum.

"Yes, Mum." Joan puts on her coat.

"Shush, Yan! Can you hear the shell?"

"We need to go. Be quick, Yan!"

"This boat will float well. See?"

"We can sing the sailing song."

"Sail, sail, sail. Look, a mermaid's tail!"

"Joan! You are wet! Get in."

"Yes, Mum!"
Joan and Yan are back.

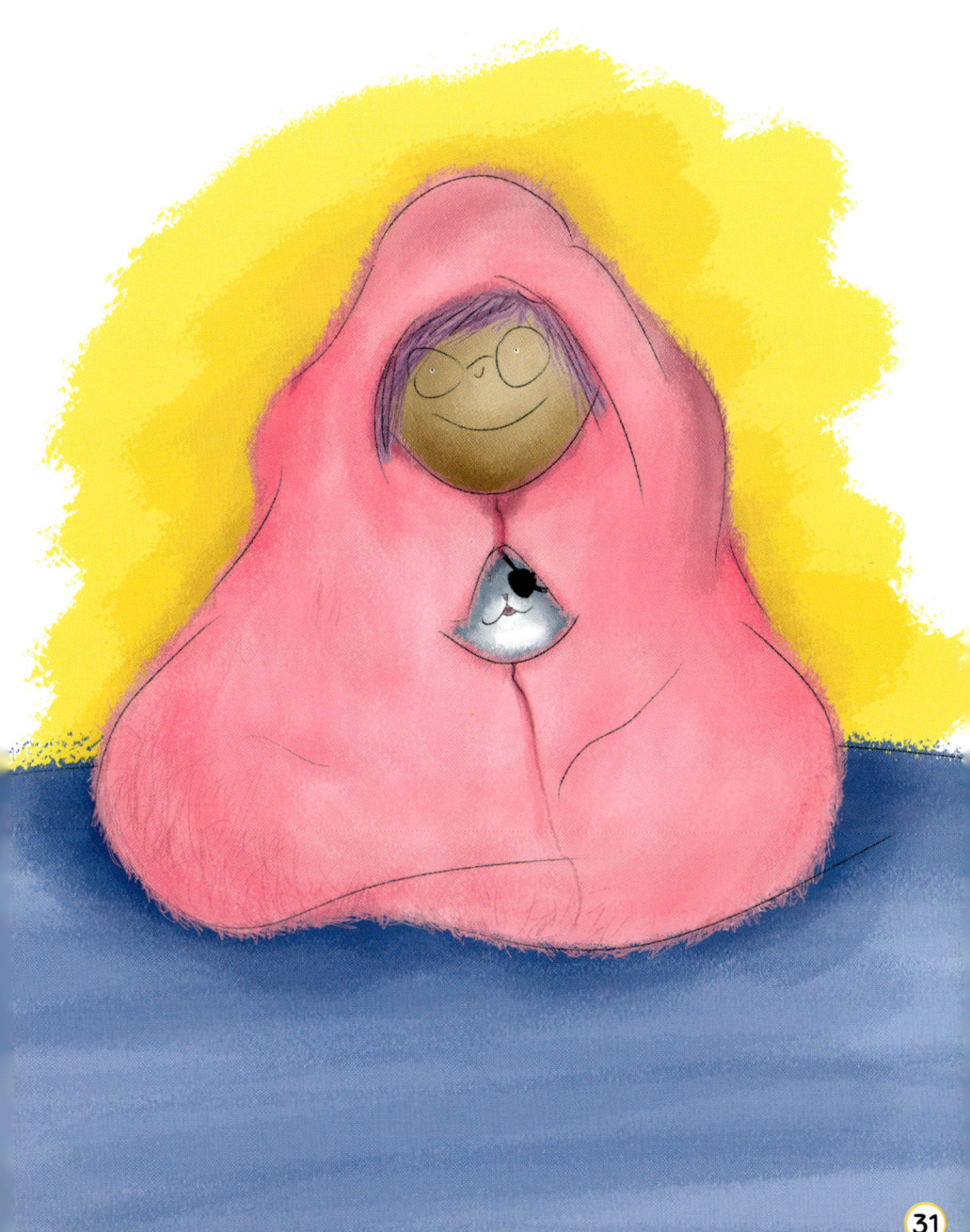

©2020 **BookLife Publishing Ltd.**
King's Lynn, Norfolk PE30 4LS

ISBN 978-1-83927-284-4
All rights reserved. Printed in Malaysia.
A catalogue record for this book is available from the British Library.

Bonza the Monster & Joan's Backyard
Written by Kirsty Holmes
Illustrated by Drue Rintoul

An Introduction to BookLife Readers...

Our Readers have been specifically created in line with the London Institute of Education's approach to book banding and are phonetically decodable and ordered to support each phase of the Letters and Sounds document.

Each book has been created to provide the best possible reading and learning experience. Our aim is to share our love of books with children, providing both emerging readers and prolific page-turners with beautiful books that are guaranteed to provoke interest and learning, regardless of ability.

BOOK BAND GRADED using the Institute of Education's approach to levelling.

PHONETICALLY DECODABLE supporting each phase of Letters and Sounds.

EXERCISES AND QUESTIONS to offer reinforcement and to ascertain comprehension.

BEAUTIFULLY ILLUSTRATED to inspire and provoke engagement, providing a variety of styles for the reader to enjoy whilst reading through the series.

AUTHOR INSIGHT:
KIRSTY HOLMES

Kirsty Holmes, holder of a BA, PGCE, and an MA, was born in Norfolk, England. She has written over 60 books for BookLife Publishing, and her stories are full of imagination, creativity and fun.

PHASE 3

This book is a 'b' level and is a yellow level 3 book band.